CPS-Peirce ES

3 24891 9800919 0

DISCARD W9-BHX-761

Looking & Feeling Good in Your Body

Poirce Library Media Center
1423 West Bryn Mawr Avenue
Chicago, Illinois 60660
(773) 534-2440

Understanding Obesity

Looking & Feeling Good in Your Body

Joan Esherick

Mason Crest

Mason Crest
450 Parkway Drive, Suite D
Broomall, PA 19008
www.masoncrest.com

Copyright © 2015 by Mason Crest, an imprint of National Highlights, Inc.
All rights reserved. No part of this publication may be reproduced or trans-
mitted in any form or by any means, electronic or mechanical, including
photocopying, recording, taping, or any information storage and retrieval
system, without permission from the publisher.

Printed in the United States of America.

Series ISBN: 978-1-4222-3056-5
ISBN: 978-1-4222-3063-3
ebook ISBN: 978-1-4222-8846-7

Cataloging-in-Publication Data on file with the Library of Congress.

Contents

KEY ICONS TO LOOK FOR:

 Text-Dependent Questions: These questions send the reader back to the text for more careful attention to the evidence presented there.

 Words to Understand: These words with their easy-to-understand definitions will increase the reader's understanding of the text, while building vocabulary skills.

 Series Glossary of Key Terms: This back-of-the book glossary contains terminology used throughout this series. Words found here increase the reader's ability to read and comprehend higher-level books and articles in this field.

 Research Projects: Readers are pointed toward areas of further inquiry connected to each chapter. Suggestions are provided for projects that encourage deeper research and analysis.

 Sidebars: This boxed material within the main text allows readers to build knowledge, gain insights, explore possibilities, and broaden their perspectives by weaving together additional information to provide realistic and holistic perspectives.

Introduction

We as a society often reserve our harshest criticism for those conditions we understand the least. Such is the case with obesity. Obesity is a chronic and often-fatal disease that accounts for 300,000 deaths each year. It is second only to smoking as a cause of premature death in the United States. People suffering from obesity need understanding, support, and medical assistance. Yet what they often receive is scorn.

Today, children are the fastest growing segment of the obese population in the United States. This constitutes a public health crisis of enormous proportions. Living with childhood obesity affects self-esteem, employment, and attainment of higher education. But childhood obesity is much more than a social stigma. It has serious health consequences.

Childhood obesity increases the risk for poor health in adulthood and premature death. Depression, diabetes, asthma, gallstones, orthopedic diseases, and other obesity-related conditions are all on the rise in children. Over the last 20 years, more children are being diagnosed with type 2 diabetes—a leading cause of preventable blindness, kidney failure, heart disease, stroke, and amputations. Obesity is undoubtedly the most pressing nutritional disorder among young people today.

This series is an excellent first step toward understanding the obesity crisis and profiling approaches for remedying it. If we are to reverse obesity's current trend, there must be family, community, and national objectives promoting healthy eating and exercise. As a nation, we must demand broad-based public-health initiatives to limit TV watching, curtail junk food advertising toward children, and promote physical activity. More than rhetoric, these need to be our rallying cry. Anything short of this will eventually fail, and within our lifetime obesity will become the leading cause of death in the United States if not in the world.

Victor F. Garcia, M.D.
Founder, Bariatric Surgery Center
Cincinnati Children's Hospital Medical Center
Professor of Pediatrics and Surgery
School of Medicine
University of Cincinnati

Words to Understand

legitimate: Reasonable, fair, acceptable.

Chapter 1

We Each Have Something

- Media Messages and Big Fat Lies

- Deeper Than Skin

- Becoming the Best We Can Be

Ladies Home Journal named her one of the Most Fascinating Women of the Year. *People* magazine picked her as one of the Most Intriguing People of the Year and included her on one of its "10 Best Dressed" lists in 1999. She won the 1998 E! Golden Hanger Award for female fashion breakthrough; the 1998 Emmy Award for Best Supporting Actress; the 1999 Golden Globe Award for Best Supporting Actress; and the 2000 Genii Award for best television in the American Women in Radio and Television category. *Glamour* magazine named her as one of their Women of the Year. Can you guess who this acclaimed American actress might be?

Contrary to what you might expect, she is not Jennifer Aniston, Julia Stiles, Demi Moore, Meryl Streep, Nicole Kidman, Meg Ryan, Jennifer Lopez, Kirsten Dunst, Cameron Diaz, Mary-Kate Olson, Ashley Olson, Courtney Cox, Julia Roberts, or Halle Berry. She's not even thin. In fact, her *New York Times* best-selling book is titled *Wake Up, I'm Fat!* (Broadway Books, 1999). Who is this award-winning artist? Her name is Camryn Manheim.

Camryn Manheim isn't just an award-winning television actress and author. She has a master's degree from New York University's Acting Program; she's performed on and off Broadway; she's acted in films; she's produced films; she's advocated for the rights of people with disabilities; she's served on the board of the American Civil Liberties Union (ACLU); and she's one of America's most vocal supporters of the size-acceptance movement. Camryn Manheim is a plus-size woman working in an industry that applauds anorexic thinness, but she found her niche and learned that she has much to contribute to this world. And the world is better for it.

But the world might never have known this talented actress or her passionate advocacy on behalf of those with disabilities.

As a teenager or young adult, Camryn Manheim could have looked in the mirror and decided, as many of us do, that she was "too big" or "too ugly" to make it in this world, especially as an actress in Hollywood, the land of pretty people. Thankfully, she didn't. She saw beyond the image in the mirror to the gifted, strong, passionate woman she was. Her journey of self-acceptance allowed her ultimately to pursue her dreams and impact those around her, and those around the world, in ways she might never have imagined—in much more important ways than being just another pretty face on the television screen. What was the key? She realized she had something worthwhile to offer, even if her body type didn't match the cultural image of a movie star. She saw herself as worthwhile and significant just the way she was.

Media Messages and Big Fat Lies

Have you ever wished you could be someone else? Have you ever looked into the mirror and thought "if only": *if only I had thicker hair; if only I had a smaller nose; if only I had clear skin, or less freckles, or a thinner face.* Or have you looked at another person and thought, *I wish I was as smart and athletic as he is,* or, *If I grew up in her family, I could be somebody, too.* If you're like most of us, you have. We've all wished to be someone else at some time in our lives. Sometimes we long to be different because of hardships we face at home or the **legitimate** desire to do greater good in this world. Many of us, however, are dissatisfied with ourselves because we've fallen prey to media messages that define importance and value as belonging only to ultrathin, ultrarich, ultrasuccessful, airbrushed beauties.

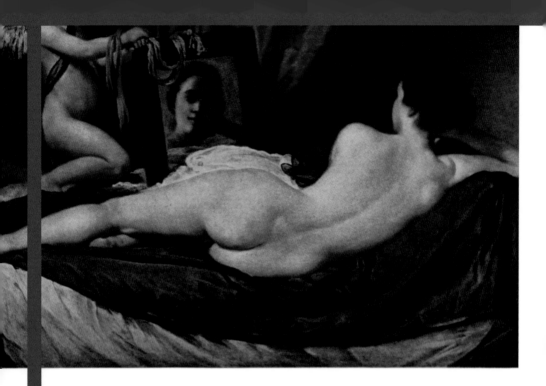

Media messages? you might wonder. *What media messages?*

Think about the last movie you saw in the theaters. What kind of people played the "good" guys, the heroes, the heroines, or the positive role models? Were any of them fat, covered with acne, disfigured, or physically challenged? Did any of them have bad hair, terrible makeup, crossed eyes, or clashing wardrobes?

Now think about your favorite television shows, commercials, and recording artists. Ask the same questions. How many of these idols are less-than-attractive people?

How about the bad guys? How do they dress? What do they look like? What about the creatures who scare us? How do they appear? How do movies portray evil? We have only to look at Freddy Krueger from the *Nightmare on Elm Street* film series or Two Face from the *Batman* films to know.

The message behind these images is this: Good guys are beautiful; bad guys are not. People who have something to offer are handsome or pretty

> *"There has been this enormous change from girls being principally concerned with good works to now being concerned with good looks as a measure of their self-worth."*
>
> *—Joan Jacobs Brumberg, author of The Body Project: An Intimate History of American Girls*

and talented; people with little to contribute are overweight, scarred, and inept. Important people are athletic, muscle-toned, tanned, and impeccably dressed; worthless people are klutzy, fat, and lazy. The message is out there, and it's deliberate.

Media (newspapers, magazines, television, movies, advertisements, etc.) exist for three reasons: to inform, to entertain, and to sell. Yes, sell. The driving force behind most media outlets is money. The people running various media outlets know that you and I, the "consumers," don't want to be reminded of our weaknesses or ugliness. We want to see beauty, power, wealth, and all the things we hope to be. Media images strive to make us believe that if we look a certain way, dress in certain clothes, become like certain stars, or own certain things we'll fulfill our dreams (get the girl or guy, find fame, acquire acceptance, prove our critics wrong, or win whatever it is we hope to win). They play to our emotions: our desires to be liked, accepted, loved, approved of, and to find purpose and meaning. If we think their product can give us these things, we'll buy it (go to the movie, purchase the CD,

**Make Connections:
The Effect of Media on Girls**

About-Face, an organization established in 1995 to combat negative and distorted images of women portrayed in the media, states on their website that

- 95 percent of girls want to lose weight
- teenage girls who read articles about dieting are five times more likely to take extreme weight-loss measures five years later than girls who do not read such articles
- body image and eating disturbances contribute to higher levels of depression in adolescent girls
- Women of color and Caucasian women are equally likely to present symptoms of eating disorders such as bulimia and binge

wear the designer label, etc.), and the media outlets will make more money. It's a strong, well-designed play for our minds and our cash.

But it's a lie.

Money can't buy love or friendship. Clothing can't make us important. Beauty can't give us meaning and purpose. Younger actresses are recognizing the impact that Hollywood has on young girls' views of their bodies. Jennifer

Lawrence, a popular actress who stars in *The Hunger Games* told *Elle* magazine, "I'm never going to starve myself for a part...I don't want little girls to be like, 'Oh, I want to look like Katniss, so I'm going to skip dinner.'"

When was the last time you found lasting happiness in a hairstyle? Hair grows back, hairstyles change. What was "beautiful" in the year 2000 isn't "in" in 2015. What was fashionable a year ago is passé now. The definition of beauty in the twenty-first century is very different than how people defined beauty a century ago.

Hairstyles aren't the only things that change. How about makeup? Does wearing the right brand of makeup satisfy our souls? How about having fuller lips or thinner eyebrows? What about clothing? Does the label inside our

Make Connections:
Beauty Through the Ages

Nineteenth-century actress and opera singer Lillian Russell, who weighed 200 pounds, was considered the "ideal" woman in the 1890s.

In the 1950s, Marilyn Monroe, at 5 feet 5½ inches tall and weighing 140 pounds, was the standard of centerfold beauty.

Just a decade after Marilyn Monroe's size 14 beauty captured America, British teenager Lesley Hornby (Twiggy) became the world's first international supermodel, and the "Twiggy" look of anorexic thinness was in.

The workout craze of the 1980s brought images of fitness as the next American beauty trend. Hollywood actress, political activist, and fitness guru Jane Fonda typified the standard of American beauty at that time.

shirts or the logo on our hats really make us more or less important than our peers? This year's hot spring designer label will be old news by the fall.

And what about, you guessed it, body weight? Do you weigh the same today as you did ten years ago? If you're currently seventeen years old, of course you don't. It would be ridiculous to compare an older teenager with a seven-year-old child. Yet we panic at age seventeen if we weigh more than we did at thirteen. We freak if our hips are bigger or our shoulders are broader—both of which are normal developmental changes we experience as we approach adulthood.

Even into adulthood we make silly comparisons. A twenty-seven-year-old who has just given birth to her first child feels worthless and unattractive because she weighs more and looks different than she did at seventeen. Absurd but true. We make these comparisons, unfair as they are, all the time. Especially when we look at ourselves. We forget that body weights and sizes, like fashions and hairstyles, change with age, circumstances, health issues, and season of life.

Yet media images would have us believe that all of these things—body size, weight, clothing styles, and facial attractiveness—are what make us important. Externals, they insist, give us meaning.

Not true! *Real* worth and *true* beauty have nothing to do with what's on the outside; these are found within us, and they can't be taken away. Because they reside inside of us, each of us can be beautiful and lead lives of significance, no matter what our appearance or body size.

Deeper Than Skin

You've heard it a million times: "Beauty is only skin deep." This old proverb reveals an important truth. True beauty, value, and significance have more to do with who we are on the inside than what we look like. What we look like changes with time; who we are stays with us.

Listen to what these famous people say about beauty and what it means to them (excerpted from interviews published in Oprah.com's feature *Beauty from the Inside Out*). When asked "What does beauty mean to you?" here's how each responded:

Country music star Wynonna Judd: "Pretty is as pretty does. Beauty to me is mind, body, spirit, where balance is the key. If you're beautiful outside but you're hateful inside, you're out of balance! I think that beauty truly comes from within. . . . It's all attitude baby! The rest is extra."

Pop singer Beyoncé Knowles: "My mom always told me that beauty fades—outside beauty fades—but inner beauty is forever."

Actress Ashley Olson: "I definitely think it's when you're happy and you feel confident. I mean, that's when your beauty really shows."

Actress Mary-Kate Olson: "When you're happy and you feel good about yourself and you can be yourself, you've got that extra glow and it shows."

Lifecoach Harriette Cole: "Beauty is feeling great from the inside out. That includes feeling healthy, strong, and vibrant . . . it's fundamentally spiritual."

Each of these famous women is beautiful in her own right, not so much because of her appearance, but because of her inner attitude. She's beautiful because she feels beautiful, and she feels beautiful because she knows her beauty, worth, and dignity are based on who she is on the inside. Even if these women's careers ended tomorrow or they were horribly scarred in car accidents or house fires, each would retain her inner beauty because it is rooted within. The same could be said for Camryn Manheim, whose story opened this chapter and whose beauty can never be taken away.

That's the saddest part of the media's lies. The media's false definitions of importance and beauty can be lost in a heartbeat: a disfiguring auto accident, a scarring assault, a financially devastating lawsuit or divorce. Circumstances and events can strip anyone—no matter who they are—of external beauty and value. When self-worth is dependent on what we look like or how much money we have, it won't last. Everyone gets old, a bit (or more) flabby, toothless, and wrinkled in time; we all get sick; we all can lose financial security or fancy things. But inner beauty and value lasts regardless of our circumstances.

That's where this book comes in.

Becoming the Best We Can Be

This book is designed to help us make the most of the bodies we've been given, no matter their size, shape, or color. How we were made, the families into which

we were born, how rich or poor we might be—these are things over which we had no say or control and for which we cannot take credit or blame. Whether we entered this world as African Americans living in affluent suburbs, Asian Americans in blue-collar inner-city neighborhoods, urban Latinos in gang-dominated territories, or rural Caucasian farmers living in the hills of rural Appalachia wasn't our choosing. We didn't get to decide our genetics-controlled hair colors, eye colors, body shapes, body sizes, skin colors, or levels

Research Project

You discovered in this chapter that being very thin was not considered attractive until the 1960s. Think about what the media labels attractive today. Then go to the library and research when this definition of beauty became popular. Create a timeline that shows when each form of beauty was popular.

of natural athletic ability. *How* we live in these bodies, however, is our choice, a choice we can make one day at a time, a choice that will enable us to feel the best we can about ourselves, and one that allows us to take advantage of the beauty within.

Text-Dependent Questions:

1. Why does the media focus so heavily on beauty, wealth, and power?
2. Why shouldn't people in their twenties or thirties compare themselves to how they looked at seventeen?
3. Why should you focus more on inner beauty than physical beauty?
4. Why shouldn't you focus on what the media defines as beauty?

Words to Understand

lupus: An autoimmune disease in which the body attacks its own cells.

bulbous: Round and swollen-looking.

egotism: Having an exaggerated sense of self-importance.

Chapter 2

Being Your Best Through Self-Confidence

- Confidence: An Overlooked Virtue

- Confidence Can Go a LONG Way!

- Kids Can Make a Difference, Too!

- How About You? Confidence Can Be Built!

He was the first person with Down syndrome to star in a weekly television series. Chris Burke, Corky on the program *Life Goes On*, transformed the public's understanding of what it means to be a person with a disability, mental or physical. He now gives inspirational speeches all over the country, is a valued member of the National Down Syndrome Society (NDSS), and is the singer in the folk band Forever Friends. His former acting career had him making special guest appearances on Emmy award-winning shows which included *ER* and *The Division*.

She was brutally attacked by a pair of razorblade-wielding assailants. The two men savagely slashed her face, she spent five days in the hospital, and her modeling career, which had just taken off, was effectively ended. For years afterward the young model suffered posttraumatic stress disorder (PTSD), debilitating depressions, and long-term anxiety, even though she served on the board of the National Center for Victims of Crime and lobbied for changes in legislation during that time. She also wrote movie scripts and worked with a movie director. Today, after successfully finding medical help for her anxiety and PTSD, the once up-and-coming model Marla Hanson, who still carries scars of her attack, is a wife, mother, inspirational speaker, and screenwriter of *The Blackout* and *Subway Stories*. Her story was made into a TV movie, *The Marla Hanson Story* in 1991.

He contracted polio as a preschooler, which permanently paralyzed his then four-year-old legs. At thirteen, he won a national talent competition. By the time he was twenty he was performing all over the world. Itzhak Perlman, the renowned violinist, has since performed with every major orchestra in the world, recorded everything from baroque to contemporary music, has been the subject of documentary programs and films, and is a well-known advocate for the rights of people with disabilities.

He was born in London and raised by his Brazilian mother and Nigerian father. As a child he contracted a form of **lupus**, which tricks the body's

immune system into believing that normal tissue is foreign tissue and needs to be attacked. His lupus, called discoid lupus, left him with obvious, **bulbous** scars beneath his eyes, but he pursued an education (a degree in architecture) and his dream of being a musician. Today, the award-winning singer/songwriter Seal has sold more than 20 million albums worldwide.

None of these individuals represents today's American standards of external beauty. All have physical differences or scars, yet each has made a niche for himself or herself in a competitive world. What do they have in common (apart from their blemishes)? Confidence.

Confidence: An Overlooked Virtue

Just what is confidence? Dictionaries define confidence as freedom from doubt; belief in yourself and your abilities; or a sense of trust in yourself or another. Thesauruses list synonyms for confidence like sureness, assuredness, or self-assurance. We often think of confidence negatively as **egotism** (too much confidence), bravado (bragging rights), or puffed-up self-esteem. These negative images of confidence are distortions. It is possible to develop confidence without becoming a stuck-up egotist. True confidence, the quiet assurance of one's dignity, ability, and usefulness, is the virtue people like Chris Burke, Marla Hanson, Itzhak Perlman, and Seal have in common. And notice this: their confidence has nothing to do with physical beauty or attributes. Their confidence is based in who they are, what they survived, the things about which they are passionate, and the contributions they thought they could bring to this world.

Confidence Can Go a LONG Way!

Do you ever think of yourself as someone who could make a difference? Most people don't. Yet the people who often make the greatest difference in this world are ordinary individuals doing extraordinary things. One such person is described in a novel by Catherine Ryan Hyde, later made into the movie *Pay It Forward*. The story describes what happens when twelve-year-old Trevor McKinney (played by Haley Joel Osment) accepts an assignment by his social studies teacher (played by Kevin Spacey) to come up with a plan to change the world.

His plan is this: He will help three people. When the three people Trevor helps ask how they can repay him, his plan is to tell them to help three other people instead. When the next three sets of three people ask the original three how to repay them, they, too, will be told to help three more. In chart form, the theory looks like this:

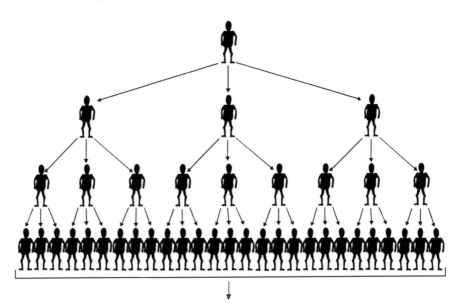

And so on, eventually impacting thousands by help-ing others three at a time.

Though Trevor's original three people aren't helped the way he envisioned, his idea becomes a national movement of good-deed doers who, instead of paying others back for kindnesses received, determine to "pay it for-ward." Trevor's idea impacts thou-sands of lives in ways the young boy could never have imagined.

When asked what her inspiration was to write *Pay It Forward*, author Catherine Ryan Hyde describes it this way:

"About twenty-five years ago, I was driving alone in a rough area of Los Angeles late at night. My poor old car was not in great con-dition. When I braked at the end of a free-way off-ramp, the engine suddenly died. All the lights went out—headlights, dash lights—and then the passenger compart-ment started to fill with smoke.

"I jumped out of the car to see two men running toward me, one holding a blanket. I had no idea that this would turn out to be 'the good news.' One of the men popped the hood of my car. My engine was on fire, the flames burning along the throttle line.

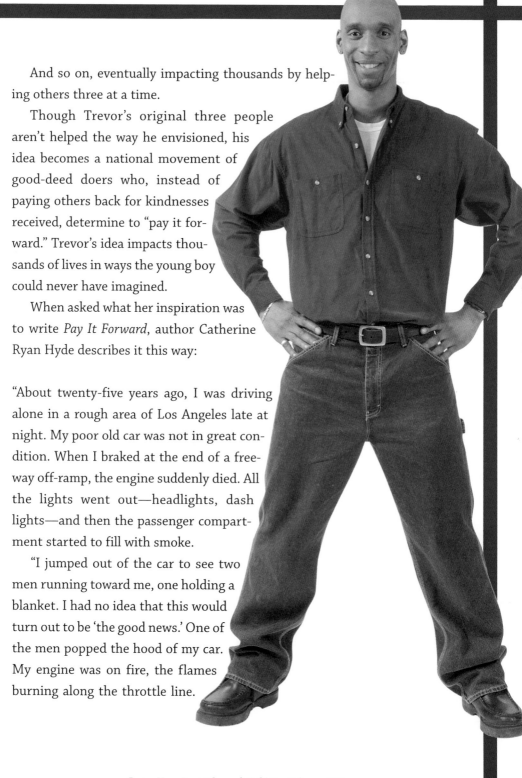

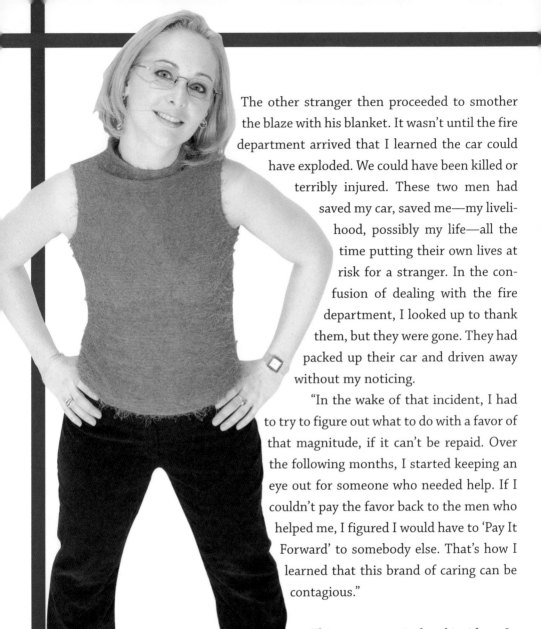

The other stranger then proceeded to smother the blaze with his blanket. It wasn't until the fire department arrived that I learned the car could have exploded. We could have been killed or terribly injured. These two men had saved my car, saved me—my livelihood, possibly my life—all the time putting their own lives at risk for a stranger. In the confusion of dealing with the fire department, I looked up to thank them, but they were gone. They had packed up their car and driven away without my noticing.

"In the wake of that incident, I had to try to figure out what to do with a favor of that magnitude, if it can't be repaid. Over the following months, I started keeping an eye out for someone who needed help. If I couldn't pay the favor back to the men who helped me, I figured I would have to 'Pay It Forward' to somebody else. That's how I learned that this brand of caring can be contagious."

This was not an isolated incident. In 1981, a quiet woman named Flo Wheatley from a small town of just over 300 citizens started making sleeping bags for the homeless out of used clothing and neckties after

Make Connections:
An Ugly Quilt

You Can Make a Difference!
For instructions on making an Ugly Quilt for the
homeless, go online to
www.uglyquilts.org
or contact

MY BROTHERS' KEEPER QUILT GROUP
RR 1 Box 1049
Hop Bottom, PA 18824 USA

recalling the kindness a homeless man showed her on a trip to New York City when she sought treatment for her young son's cancer. Mrs. Wheatley's husband traveled from their rural home in northeastern Pennsylvania to New York on business several times a year. By 1982, after only a year, the young mother had handmade eight quilts that her husband delivered in person to people living on the streets of New York.

Word spread of her efforts, and soon cartons of used clothing were being dropped at her doorstep. She recruited friends and family and formed the My Brothers' Keeper Quilt Group. A local pastor's wife invited her to speak at church and to demonstrate how she made what would later be called

"Ugly Quilts." And word spread. Mrs. Wheatley's story appeared in national magazines, and these quilts for the homeless soon became the favorite project of public schools, scout and civic organizations, church groups, and shelter volunteers all over the nation. By 1995, over five thousand Ugly Quilts were being distributed annually all over America to individuals who live on the nation's streets, and they are still being distributed to this day, 30 years after Mrs. Wheatley made the first one!

This one woman, from a very small town, had confidence that she could do something to help someone else. By repaying the kindness of the homeless man who helped her with kindness to other homeless people, this one woman (and the man who first helped her) effectively helped thousands. Her confidence and desire to help others contributed far more to this world than glamour and skin-deep beauty ever will.

Flo Wheatley's contribution began by embracing who she was (a woman from a small town whose husband traveled to New York), acknowledging her talents and skills (her ability to sew), and using what she had (old clothes) to make a difference in the life of one homeless person. One became eight, which in turn became thousands. Her confidence allowed her to make the most of who she was and to change the world one homeless person at a time.

Kids Can Make a Difference, Too!

Adults aren't the only ones who can make a difference. Youth Making a Difference (YMAD) is a nonprofit organization that is based in Utah. High-school aged teens volunteer and go on "expeditions" that take place over Thanksgiving or Spring Break. They go to places all over the world and perform a range of tasks, from teaching English and newborn infant care to painting schools and donating clothing and supplies. Students go through a ten month training program before they go off on an expedition, and must raise $3,700 through fundraising. This money helps pay for the training, flights, evacuation insurance, transportation, lodging, and meals for the expedition.

In most cases, all it takes is for someone to have an idea, the confidence, and the will to make the most of who they are (their talents, resources, and abilities). In each case, lives were changed.

How About You? Confidence Can Be Built!

Oh, I could never do something like that. No, those are the exceptions; I'm just an ordinary person with ordinary abilities. I can't really make a difference.

Sound familiar?

It should. Most people, especially in their teen years, think this way. But some people overcome these doubts and move forward to make a difference. How? The answer begins with self-confidence. How's your self-confidence level? When you think about yourself, what do you think? Do you tend to put yourself down, or can you honestly assess what you *can* do and embrace it as part of who you are?

If you tend to put yourself down, or lack self-esteem, try these things to boost your confidence level:

1. Be realistic. No one is really *all* bad or a complete screwup. We all have things we do well and things we don't do as well as others. Don't think in terms of all-or-nothing.
2. Turn off the self-put-down voice. Every time you're tempted to tell yourself how fat, ugly, or incapable you are, pretend that those thoughts are part of a prerecorded message on a bad tape. Imagine turning the tape player off every time one of those thoughts pops

into your head. Silence your self-criticism; it's probably not true anyway.

3. Make a list of things other people, especially people you respect (friends, parents, coaches, religious leaders, former teachers, etc.), say you do well or like about you. Keep that list in your wallet and read it every time you begin to doubt yourself.

4. Write down anything you do well. Maybe you know how to be a friend. Maybe you can help others calm down when they're upset. Maybe you can smile even when life gets you down. Maybe you can bake great cookies or write encouraging letters. Maybe you're a good student, a talented musician, or someone who can draw cartoons really well. Whatever it is, write it down and refer to it often.

5. Stop comparing yourself to other people. You are unique. You have something to offer this world that is all your own. No one sees things quite the same way as you do. No one has your same set of experiences, memories, or family dynamics. Only you can offer your opinion or perspective on things. You are unique and you are needed.

Research Project

Go online and research what charities and organizations are in your area that focus on helping people in need. Are there more than you were expecting? What kind of work do they do? Maybe they make things, like "Ugly Quilts," or maybe they collect food donations to give out to people who are hungry. Create a map of your area, marking where each of these organizations or charities is located.

6. Stop condemning yourself for mistakes or faults. Everyone makes mistakes. We all have weaknesses. They are nothing to be ashamed of; it's just part of being human. Our strengths and weaknesses are part of what make us who we are. They are what make us need each other. What a boring world we'd live in if everyone were perfect.

7. Look at your failures and embarrassments as opportunities to grow and change. Learn to see them with a sense of humor. Remember, *everyone* experiences moments of failure or shame. We can learn from these events and become better for them.

8. Make a list of your interests. What do you like doing? What interests you? If you could do anything or be anyone, what would it be? Your interests, dreams, and passions are part of your uniqueness, too.

9. Do something new. Volunteer to help others. Try rock climbing or rappelling. Write a letter to your local paper. Step outside your comfort zone. Stretch your boundaries.

10. Take care of yourself—mind, body, and soul. Get enough sleep; exercise regularly; eat right; take time to laugh; treat yourself now and

**Make Connections:
Build Confidence by Volunteering!**

Try volunteering at one of these dozen places to boost your self-confidence:

your public library
a hospital children's ward
a local soup kitchen
your church, synagogue, mosque, or other
   religious organization
a local civic organization's carnival or fair
an animal shelter, rescue organization, or
   veterinary clinic
a summer recreation program
a recycling center
Special Olympics
state or county parks
a nursing home or senior center
Red Cross, United Way, or other national helping
   agency

then; do things to encourage your spiritual life; surround yourself with people who are *good* for you and will encourage your dreams.

If you try the above and put some of them into regular practice, your confidence level *will* grow: not the false confidence we find in arrogant, full-of-

Text-Dependent Questions:

1. Explain what "pay it forward" means.
2. What should you try to do every time you think a negative thought about yourself?
3. Why shouldn't you compare yourself to peers or people you see in the media?
4. List two ways you should view your failures or embarrassing moments.

themselves people, but the confidence that comes from knowing who you are, realizing your strengths and limitations, and being assured of your ability to make a difference, even if it's in the life of only one other person. You really can impact your world!

What's stopping you? Confidence is only one look inside ourselves away. Perhaps, however, you look and don't like what you see. Then work on changing the things that can be changed and accept the rest as part of what makes you uniquely you. Focus on your strengths and abilities.

Maybe, however, other issues are undermining your inner confidence. Maybe what you see on the outside is making you feel worse inside. What do we do then?

The next several chapters focus on specific things we can do to make the most of what we see in the mirror (our hair, complexion, body type, clothing styles, etc.). Like it or not, we live in a visual world. Sometimes what we view with our eyes can impact how we feel. If we like, or at least accept, what we see in the mirror, it can help us celebrate who we are beneath our skin.

Words to Understand

nodules: Small masses of cells or tissues.

dermatology: The branch of medicine that deals with skin and skin diseases.

nonabrasive: Gentle; something that does not use friction and roughness of texture to smooth an area.

rehydrate: To return moisture to something, for example, the skin.

ocher: A brownish-yellow color.

genetic: Relating to the transfer of some characteristic through genes.

follicle: A small anatomical sac.

Chapter 3

Making the Most of Your Body with Skin Care and Cover-Ups

- Tip #1: Improve the Overall Health of Your Skin

- Tip #2: Soften the Look of Moles and Blemishes

- Tip #3: Reduce the Look of Scars or Cover Minor Skin Irregularities

- Tip #4: Remove Excess Hair Growth

It's so much easier to live with imperfections that others can't see!

Just ask actresses Cameron Diaz, Miley Cyrus, and Megan Fox; actors Daniel Radcliffe and Brad Pitt; or singer Adam Lambert. Each of these celebrities knows firsthand the frustration and long-term effects of dealing with acne, an inflammatory skin disease marked by clogged pores, blackheads, pimples, pus-filled lesions called pustules, **nodules**, and cysts. Severe acne can leave the skin grooved and scarred for life.

Skin problems, when restricted to areas of the body normally covered by clothing, rarely undermine self-esteem or confidence. But when skin issues become visible or involve our face and hands, we may find ourselves becoming uncomfortable and self-conscious. Fifteen-year-old Adrianna describes it this way:

I used to get breakouts on my chin and on the sides of my face. Whenever my acne actively erupted, I found myself wearing my hair down and tilting my head so that my hair covered the latest pimples. I didn't really want to look at anyone or make eye contact. As long as I kept my head down, my hair covered my acne pretty well. I was just so self-conscious. I felt like all that other people could see was my ugly skin. But when my face cleared up, I felt like I could go back to being the regular me.

Twelve-year-old Josh, who has eczema (a condition marked by itchy, raised red patches of skin) on his elbows and knees, felt similarly to Adrianna:

My eczema was always worst in the winter. Then it sometimes got really bad; it looked really gross. It actually looked worse than it felt, but I didn't really care. I didn't think about what other people thought because my arms and legs were always covered. Then, in my sophomore year of high school, we had to take winter swimming. It was a mandatory class for every tenth-grader. All of a sudden the big crusty

patches on my arms and legs became an issue. People must have thought I was contagious or something. I started noticing kids looking at the red, leathery patches on my arms and legs. Even my friends. All I wanted to do was hide.

Josh and Adrianna's skin conditions, when they became visible, kept them from feeling confident and acting like themselves, even around their friends.

Acne, though common, is only one of many skin problems that can rob us of confidence. The American Academy of **Dermatology** is an organization that has been around for 75 years and provides people with information about conditions that relate to the skin, hair, and nails. Most of us are familiar with these conditions. Once-normal childhood diseases like chickenpox and measles, for example, caused itchy lesions or pockmarks on the skin. Allergies still cause rashes or hives. HIV and AIDS cause a condition called Kaposi's sarcoma, a cancer-like disease causing purple lesions to form on the skin. Seal, the London-born pop singer described in the last chapter, has a disease called lupus that affects his skin and scars his face. In addition to diseases, scars, moles, blemishes, birthmarks, or differences in skin pigmentation (different colored splotches of skin) can also make us feel inferior or ashamed. Even minor, temporary skin difficulties can shatter our confidence.

Sixteen-year-old Amber looked forward to attending her first high-school formal until a huge (in her mind) zit developed on the very tip of her nose three days before the special date. Once thrilled about how she looked in her gown and full of confidence about attending, the teenager decided she couldn't go. She couldn't bear the thought of everyone looking at the "witch's bump" protruding from the center of her face.

Okay. Granted. Amber's reaction may seem extreme, but it's very real. How she looked on the outside, in particular how her face looked, impacted how she felt on the inside.

What can we do to improve the condition and appearance of our skin? Try the following tips to improve your skin condition and boost your self-confidence!

Tip #1: Improve the Overall Health of Your Skin

As Rona Berg, the former beauty editor of the *New York Times Magazine*, states in her book *Beauty: The New Basics* (Workman Publishing, 2001), "the skin holds no secrets. If the eyes are the mirror of the soul, the skin is the body's lie detector." Skin doesn't lie. The skin's condition communicates quite a bit about the body's overall health. When we're tired, the skin beneath our eyes darkens and droops. When we're under pressure or feeling stress, the skin on our foreheads and around our eyes develops creases. When we're sick, we look pale, gray, or flush. When we don't eat properly, our skin may dry out and flake. Healthy skin begins with a healthy body.

To improve our skin's health, we need to first look at our health and fitness habits. Do we eat properly? Do we get regular exercise? Are we getting the vitamins and nutrients we need? Are we drinking enough water? Basic fitness and sound nutritional strategies will give our skin the foundation it needs to look healthy.

Hygiene is a second consideration. Are we bathing regularly? Do we wash our faces daily? Are we careful to use gentle, **nonabrasive** facial cleansers? No matter what our cleansing practices have been in the past, it's never too late to begin a healthy hygiene regimen. And our skin will respond to its new pampering.

When thinking about skin hygiene, it's important to remember that not all skin is the same. Some skin is naturally dry (feels tight, can be red or flaky); some is oily (feels greasy, can appear shiny); some is extrasensitive (reddens easily, is prone to rashes, and is more sun sensitive), and some is what we call "normal" (generally healthy, even in color and texture, not splotchy). Knowing what kind of skin you have can help you better care for your skin. If you have dry skin, be sure to use a moisturizing facial wash to clean your skin. If you have oily skin, use facial cleansers designed to dry up the excess oil on your skin. For every skin type there is a skin cleanser (usually not soap) designed specifically for the issues connected with that type of skin. Be sure to use the type of skin cleanser best suited to your skin type.

No matter what skin type you have, most dermatologists recommend a four-step skin-care process for encouraging healthy skin: cleanse (to remove dirt and oils from your skin), exfoliate (to remove dead and dying skin cells to make way for new, healthy ones), moisturize (to add moisture to your skin to protect it from dryness), and use sunscreen (to protect your skin from the sun).

For Healthy Facial Skin Don't Do These Things!

1. Never squeeze, pop, or pick at blackheads, whiteheads, or other pimples.

2. Don't aggressively scrub your face or use abrasive soaps.

3. Don't overwash your face or wash it too frequently.

4. Don't unnecessarily touch your face or rest your face or chin regularly on your hands.

5. Don't rub or scratch your face.

Tip #2: Soften the Look of Moles and Blemishes

Even the best skin-care regimen won't protect us from an occasional blemish or hide birthmarks. To keep confident when blemishes or moles threaten our self-esteem, we can either learn to accept these distinguishing marks as part of our unique and individual beauty, develop techniques to cover or camouflage them using makeup, or have them surgically removed. Since surgery is called for only in extreme, disfiguring cases, we won't look at that option here. And because learning to accept moles and blemishes as part of our image is an internal process related to building confidence, which is discussed in the last chapter, we won't discuss that option at length here, either. Instead we will focus on camouflaging our facial imperfections.

It's important to realize, however, that how we handle blemishes on our faces, in part, depends on how we—and society—view them in general. We didn't always view them as needing to be covered. In decades past, blemishes were considered attractive, even desirable. Small, dark facial moles, or "beauty marks" as they were called, became distinguishing characteristics of famous actresses throughout the twentieth century. Elizabeth Taylor, Goldie Hawn, Liza Minelli, Geena Davis, and more recently, Eva Mendes, Gillian Anderson, Natalie Portman, and Alicia Silverstone all have facial moles, and none see the need to hide them. Their facial blemishes didn't undermine their confidence or their careers at all. Even today, some people consider facial moles attractive. It's a matter of individual style and taste.

Others, however, prefer to hide their beauty marks. For decades, makeup artists have skillfully hidden the natural blemishes of other celebrities from the camera. Using the same techniques, the average person can successfully hide her own blemishes. All it takes is a little knowledge of makeup.

Facial makeup comes in four basic categories: foundation, concealer, blush, and powder. Add eye makeup (eye shadow, eyeliner, and mascara) and lipstick, and you have the complete makeup set.

Foundation is the most effective type of makeup for covering moles and blemishes and evening out your skin tones. It comes in oil-based or water-based liquids or creams. The right foundation covers just about anything on your skin you might not want others to see: freckles, small birthmarks, moles, color blotches, etc. It shouldn't streak or change color when you put it on. Once applied, the right foundation should match your natural skin tone; you shouldn't be able to tell where the foundation stops and your natural skin starts. And it should feel comfortable on your face.

Which foundation you choose depends on your skin color, your skin type (dry, oily, normal), and what you're trying to cover (some foundations provide more coverage than others). Experiment with different types until you get the right one. Make sure that whatever you choose looks natural—as much like your skin as possible—and suits your skin type. A foundation ill-suited to your skin type will irritate your skin. And the wrong foundation for your skin tone can make you look like a dummy in a wax museum—something that will undermine your confidence even more than what you sought to cover in the first place.

Tip #3: Reduce the Look of Scars or Cover Minor Skin Irregularities

Severe scarring can be a debilitating, life-altering condition that cannot be covered within the scope of this book. Plastic surgery, skin grafts, and other invasive medical procedures are often necessary to reduce severe facial scars.

Minor scars, however—like the scar on your cheek from where you ran into the kitchen counter as a three-year-old, or on your chin from when you fell off your bike, or on your nose from when you picked a chicken pox lesion—can be handled easily with special makeup designed for these imperfections. Many of these scars can be visibly reduced by scar-healing creams found at your local pharmacy. Some need only light treatment with a good, skin-type-appropriate foundation. But other, darker scars may need something more.

Makeup artist Deborah Grayson, a beauty columnist at ivillage.com, was asked how to best cover dark scars. She suggests a product called Dermacolor, a specially formulated cream designed to cover scars, burns, and bruises so they become virtually unnoticeable. This cream can be used anywhere on the face and body, and it contains moisturizers to **rehydrate** the skin, which is especially important for dry facial skin. Ms. Grayson recommends DermaColor also because it comes in several shades including realistic skin tones ranging from yellow beiges to **ocher**. There are many similar products available, so experiment until you find the one that works best for you.

Tip #4: Remove Excess Hair Growth

Do you remember jokes about "unibrow" or "gorilla girl"? If not, you probably never knew someone who

Research Project

Does something about your skin embarrass you? Maybe you feel like you get a lot of pimples. Or maybe you have eczema and are self-conscious about red patches on your skin. Now go online and find celebrities that have struggled with this same problem. What did they do to cover or fix their skin? Did they use a certain type of facewash? Did they have a specific cream that they put on their arms and legs? Did they have to use foundation to cover it up?

had excessive hair growth challenges. Most teenagers don't have difficulty with excess hair unless they have underlying **genetic** or hormonal conditions. Still, many adolescents, especially girls, fret about the shape of their eyebrows or any sign of hair on their upper lips.

Although tempting and what at first might appear to be an "easy fix," do not shave or pluck facial hair. Plucking can do damage to the hair **follicle**, and, according to children's health researcher Rachel C. Vreeman and assistant professor of pediatrics Aaron E. Carrol, "shaved hair lacks the finer taper seen at the ends of unshaven hair, giving an impression of coarseness. Similarly the new hair has not yet been lightened by the sun or other chemical exposures, resulting in an appearance that seems darker than existing hair."

Cosmetologists usually recommend either waxing (spreading a thin layer of cosmetic wax over an area of hair growth, allowing it to cool or set, then removing the wax, which pulls the hair with it), electrolysis (using electricity to kill the hair root), or using depilatory creams like Surgi-Cream or Nair, which melt away hair via a chemical reaction between the ingredients in the

Text-Dependent Questions:

1. How does the skin reveal how healthy a person is?
2. List the four-step skin-care process.
3. What causes hair that was shaved to look darker when growing back?
4. Why do most cosmetologists recommend waxing, electrolysis, or depilatory creams for hair removal?

cream and the structure of your hair. Waxing pulls the hair out below the skin's surface, but doesn't damage the hair follicle, and only needs to be done every three to five weeks. Electrolysis can be expensive and tedious. Improperly done, scarring can occur and the hair can grow back. Properly done means permanently being hair-free. Depilatory creams only remove hair at the surface, can actually burn the skin if left on too long, and must be reapplied every few days.

However you choose to accomplish it, excess hair removal can help you feel better about your appearance every bit as much as covering blemishes or reducing scars. The goal, however, isn't physical perfection; it's becoming more comfortable with how you look so you can feel more confident inside. The right makeup and hairstyles can also build our confidence and self-esteem.

Make Connections:
To Pluck, Shave, Wax, or Cream?

Here's the scoop on the most common methods of removing unwanted hair. Knowing a bit about each technique will help you pick what works for you. Make sure you don't jump into plucking, shaving, or waxing without knowing what you're doing!

Plucking (using tweezers or your fingertips to forcibly "pluck" individual hairs):

It's cheap, convenient, can be painful, can leave the skin red and irritated, and causes hair follicle damage. Plucking needs to be frequently repeated.

Shaving (using a razor to remove unwanted hair at the skin's surface):

Like plucking, it's cheap, can be painful, and can irritate the skin. Shaving costs include the price of a razor, replacement blades, and shaving creams designed to reduce shaving irritation. Shaved hair is cut off at the skin's surface and grows back quickly. Shaving must be repeated every few days to keep the skin hair-free.

Waxing (applying hot or cold wax to areas of hair removal, allowing the wax to cool or set, then peeling the wax off, which removes underlying hair with it):

Waxing is more expensive than plucking or shaving (an upper lip wax job alone can cost $7 to $17), it hurts, and is more inconvenient. But its effects last much longer, and it's a generally safe method of hair removal. Waxing only has to be repeated every three to five weeks because the hair is pulled out below the skin's surface.

Using Depilatory Creams (using chemical products to dissolve hair):

This process is expensive because it has to be repeated often, it can leave your skin burned or irritated, it can smell terrible, and it is inconvenient to use. Though easy to apply, depilatory creams can cause serious complications if used on broken, cracked, or peeling skin, near the eyes, or immediately after a facial peel. When used carefully and according to directions, these creams can be a fast, easy-to-access method of short-term hair removal.

Chapter 4

Making the Most of Your Body with Makeup and Hairstyles

- Makeup Basics for Every Body Type

- In Pursuit of Confidence-Building Hair

- Above All Be Comfortable

In 1987, a doctor faced a dilemma. A patient's cancer treatments had left her bald and gaunt-looking. Her posttreatment, death-warmed-over appearance itself wasn't unusual. What was unusual was the level of the woman's resulting depression and self-imposed isolation. The young cancer patient had become so self-conscious that she wouldn't leave her hospital room. Her doctor wanted to help her, but didn't know how.

He contacted Ed Kavanaugh, the president of the Cosmetic, Toiletry, and Fragrance Association (CTFA) and asked how he could help his struggling cancer patient. Could a professional makeover help? Because of Mr. Kavanaugh's position with the CTFA, he was able to find companies that were willing to donate appropriate cosmetics and a makeup artist who was willing to work with the woman to teach her makeup techniques and hairstyle tricks (using wigs and scarves) to help her feel beautiful again.

The cancer patient's subsequent makeover did far more than either her doctor or Ed Kavanaugh expected. The makeover not only changed the woman's physical appearance; it changed her feelings about herself, her outlook, and her view of the future she faced. She even began to feel better physically.

How this woman *felt* about how she looked affected her health and self-esteem. It wasn't her appearance that made the difference; it was how she felt about her appearance.

After hearing of the patient's dramatic improvement, the CTFA leader approached other leaders in the cosmetic industry about the opportunity they had to make a difference in cancer patients' lives. The CTFA, together with the American Cancer Society and National Cosmetology Association, soon launched a makeover program called Look Good . . . Feel Better. This nonprofit public service program now serves thousands of cancer patients throughout the world.

Look Good . . . Feel Better operates on the assumption that if we feel better about how we look, we will feel better about other things, too. Isn't that true for us all?

Think about the last time you wore a new outfit or sported a new hairstyle. Didn't you *feel* better (more confident or self-assured, perhaps)? Researchers have documented this connection between how we feel about our appearance and our levels of confidence. The better we feel about how we look, the more confident we tend to feel.

In this chapter and the next, we look at specific makeup, hairstyle, and clothing techniques we can use to make ourselves look our best and feel more confident. (Guys can check out from this chapter and skip to chapter 5).

Makeup Basics for Every Body Type

We learned in the previous chapter that effective makeup includes foundations, concealers, powders, eye makeup, and lipstick. But did you know these should be put on in a certain order? Foundation should always come first, followed by concealer, then eye makeup (eye shadow, eyeliner, mascara, in that order), then blush or rouge, followed by powder or glitter. Lipstick or lip gloss is always last.

Having the correct tools to apply your makeup can help you get a more professional look. Basic brushes for applying blush, powder, and eye shadow are available most places where cosmetics are sold. Blush brushes are soft, full-bristled, medium-sized brushes with rounded tips. Powder brushes look just like blush brushes only bigger (almost twice the size). Small, tapered, pencil-sized brushes for smoothing or detailing lipstick are also widely available. Each of these brushes allows you to more evenly and cleanly apply your makeup. They allow you to erase makeup lines and to blend the edges of your

The Order of Makeup
foundation
concealer or cover sticks
eye makeup (eye shadow, then
    eyeliner, then mascara)
blush or rouge
powder or glitter
lipstick or lip gloss

Make Connections:
The Four C's of Cosmetics

Beauty expert and author Rona Berg cites four C-words to successfully using makeup:

Comfort: How much makeup feels comfortable to you?

Color: Stick to one color family for lip, blush, and eye makeup. Use warm tones with other warm tones and cool tones with cool. Don't try to mix them.

Contour: Use brushes to smooth makeup lines and to blend edges into your natural skin. Try for natural contours.

Confidence: Makeup application isn't difficult to learn; it just takes practice. Do what you think looks good (not what friends or salespeople say) and you'll feel great. Trust your instincts! At the very least you know you can always wash it off.

makeup into the natural tones of your skin. And remember—one of the keys to natural-looking makeup is to blend, blend, blend.

Having the right brushes and putting on your makeup in the right order, though important, won't help you if you don't know what makeup styles help you look your best. What works on a round face will not work on a narrow face. What works on a high forehead will not work on a narrow brow. To discover the makeup tips best suited to your face, you might want to try a free consultation with a makeup professional at a local department store or makeup supplier (for example, Mary Kay or Avon). You might also consider hosting a makeover party for a Mary Kay consultant or a local cosmetologist.

If these options are not available to you, the following general rules will help:

1. Only use makeup to enhance your existing features (don't use it to try to add things that aren't there).

2. When you apply makeup, follow your natural facial lines and angles (your cheekbones, your nose and chin lines, the shape of your eye sockets, your lip curves, etc.).

3. For a fresh, clean-looking appearance use softer colors on your lips and rosy colors on your cheeks.

4. For a strong, assertive look, use robust lip colors and darker eye shadows.

5. For a natural look, use makeup tones that best mimic your skin tones (mauves, berries, plums, etc.). Avoid heavy eye makeup.

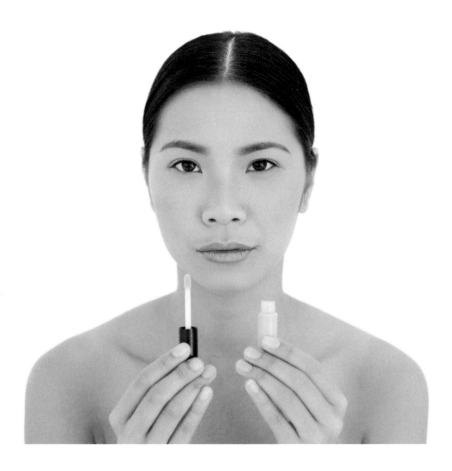

Making the Most of Your Body with Makeup and Hairstyles / 61

6. To be bold or trendy, try using foundations, blushes, lipsticks, and eye shadows of the same color family (called the "mono-chromatic" or "one-color" approach).

7. With eye shadow, contrast the shadow color with your eye color. If you have blue eyes, don't use blue shadow. If you have green eyes, avoid greens. For blue eyes try shadows in shades of brown or copper instead. For green eyes try salmon or mauve. For dark brown eyes, try honey or peach tones. For light brown eyes, use slate blue or plum. You'll be amazed at how much richer your natural eye color

Cosmetics Can Be Dangerous
Can you guess the most common makeup-related injury?
It's eye scratches (cornea and otherwise) that result when a person applying mascara scratches her eye with the mascara wand.

Make Connections: Cosmetic Safety Tips from the FDA

The U.S. Food and Drug Administration provides these safety tips to ensure safe, healthy use of cosmetics:

- Avoid using eye cosmetics if you have an eye infection or the skin around the eye is inflamed. Wait until the area is healed. Discard any eye cosmetics you were using when you got the infection.
- Don't share your cosmetics. Another person's bacteria may be hazardous to you.
- Discard dried-up mascara. Don't add saliva or water to moisten it. The bacteria from your mouth may grow in the mascara and cause infection. Adding water may introduce bacteria and will dilute the preservative that is intended to protect against microbial growth.
- Don't store cosmetics at temperatures above 85 degrees F. Cosmetics held for long periods in hot cars, for example, are more susceptible to deterioration of the preservative.
- Avoid color additives that are not approved for use in the area of the eye, such as "permanent" eyelash tints and kohl. Be especially careful to keep kohl away from children, since reports have linked it to lead poisoning.

looks when you use a contrasting eye shadow.

8. When choosing a blush color, think of what your cheeks look like after you've exercised for twenty minutes. Your best blush colors will be no darker than your postexercise flush; they may even be slightly lighter. Anything darker will look forced and fake.

9. To apply blush, redder is not better (too much red makes you look clownish). Again, the goal is to highlight your existing features. Try this trick for natural-looking blush: Smile a wide grin (show your teeth). Next, using a blush brush, lightly apply blush to the portions of your cheeks that bulge out when you smile (toward the outside of the bulge). Relax your grin, and then lightly stroke your blush from your smile bulges along your cheekbones toward your temples. The effect makes for a narrower-looking face.

10. Remember, with almost all makeup, less is more. In other words, less makeup can give you a better, more effective look than too much or heavily applied makeup can. This is especially true when applying foundation, eye shadow, and mascara.

Don't be intimidated by makeup. Think of it as a tool—a new type of crayon. Experiment with colors and techniques. Practice, practice, practice. And don't be afraid or ashamed to ask for help and advice.

The right makeup, even correctly applied, won't help us much if we feel awful about our hairstyle. Finding the right hairstyle is a bit more complicated than it seems at first. But this, like applying makeup, is something we can learn. We just need to discover some tricks of the trade.

In Pursuit of Confidence-Building Hair

Attractive hair, like attractive skin, begins with good hygiene. Good hair hygiene involves three basic steps: washing (keeping your hair clean), conditioning (keeping your hair soft and moisturized), and

Make Connections: Four Tips for Healthier Hair

According to an article in *Daily Glow*, to keep your hair healthy follow these four steps:

1. Get your hair cut and trimmed regularly.

2. Wash your hair regularly with a clarifying shampoo.

3. Always condition your hair after shampooing.

4. Deeply hydrate your hair with a leave-in conditioning treatment.

combing or brushing (detangling your hair and spreading natural oils the entire length of your hair). Choose a shampoo that is best suited to your hair type and condition. If you have dry or damaged hair, use a shampoo marked "for dry or damaged hair." If you have oily hair, use a shampoo labeled for "oily" hair. If you have thin hair, try a "volumizing" shampoo (one that is supposed to add volume to fine hair). Choose your conditioners the same way.

Make your choices based on the condition of your hair *now* (not how it was last swimming season or how it was when you had it permed four years ago).

Once you've got hair hygiene under control, it's time to think about hairstyle. Three factors most influence the best hairstyle choices: hair type and texture, face shape, and body type. Is your hair naturally straight or curly? Is it fine, coarse, thick, or thin? How about your face? Is it round, oval, square, triangular, oblong, or heart-shaped? What about your body type? Are you small framed or big boned? Do you have a long body and short legs or a short body with long legs? Are you tall, short, or just average in height? Are you slim with sharp, clearly defined facial features, or are you overweight with round features?

Here's what hairstyles work best for different facial shapes and hair features:

Round face: short, layered cuts; side parts; long straight cuts layered around the face.

Oval face: layers that frame the face; soft bangs; fuller cuts; almost any style.

Square face (boxy chin): hair length below or above the jawline; off-center layers, fringy cuts.

Triangular face (small chin): cuts that are fuller over the cheekbones and jawline; piled or upswept styles that direct attention above the eye line.

Heart-shaped face (broad forehead, narrow chin): wavy or curly styles, tousled layers, styles that add fullness around the neck.

Oblong face: side parts, layered cuts, and styles that add volume to the sides of your face.

Fine hair: super short cuts or bobs.

Thick hair: blunt-cut, mid-length bob, layered long hair.

Wavy hair: layering where the natural wave falls; thinning to reduce volume.

Curly hair: layering according to the hair's natural shape; super-short cuts; one length.

Don't forget your body type! Generally, shorter haircuts will make you look heavier, so avoid short-short cuts if you are overweight. Shorter cuts with layering on top, however, can give you the illusion of more height and make you look taller. If you are short, consider a height-inducing effect in your hair style choice. Short hairstyles almost always work best for short

Find Your Face Shape!

To determine the general shape of your face, try this trick. Look in a mirror. Then, with a water-based, nonpermanent marker or transparency pen, trace the outline of your face (not including your hair) onto the mirror. Just draw around the image you see reflected at you. Now step back. Which of these shapes does the outline you drew on the mirror most resemble: round, square, triangular (an upside down triangle), oblong, or oval? That's your face shape!

Research Project

Outline the face of your shape in a mirror, as suggested on page 67. Once you have determined what shape your face is, go online and see what makeup tips and hairstyles are recommended for someone with your facial shape. Is there a certain brush stroke you should be using? Will longer or shorter hair compliment your face more? Write down the different tips and suggestions and try them out the next time you put on makeup or get a new hairstyle.

women. Also, hair cut longer on one side or pulled to one side in a barrette or comb can help shorter women appear taller. Super-short fringy cuts work well for tall, angularly featured body types. Again, when choosing a hairstyle, consider not just your hair type and face shape, but your overall body appearance, too.

Think about what you like and what suits your fashion tastes and lifestyle. Are you a person who enjoys fussing with your hair every day? If so, choose a hairstyle that allows you to fuss to your heart's content. Are you an active athlete who doesn't have the time or desire to work at styling your hair each day? Go for a low-maintenance cut that allows you to "wash'n'wear." Do you prefer trendsetting clothing? Then your hair should be trendy, too. Do you like the wrinkled look? Go for a shaggy, messy hairstyle. Are you old-fashioned and tailored in your clothing choices? Then a classic haircut might suit you best.

Whatever your choice, your hairstyle should fit your personality, clothing styles, and lifestyle.

Text-Dependent Questions:

1. Why was Look Good...Feel Better created?
2. List the different eye shadow colors you should try if you have blue, green, or brown eyes.
3. Why shouldn't you add saliva or water to your mascara to moisten it?
4. What three things should you consider when deciding which hairstyle suits you?

Above All Be Comfortable

Think about your comfort zone, too. What hairstyle would you be comfortable living in for the next several months (or years)? What hairstyle feels the most like "you"? Which hairstyle best reflects your personality and values? In what hairstyle could you feel most confident?

There's that word again. Confidence. What hairstyle helps you feel your best? Which allows you to be the best "you" you know how to be?

Yes, consider your hair texture, head shape, body type, and clothing styles, but none of these is very important if you end up with a hairstyle you hate or don't feel attractive in.

So, what hairstyle do *you* like for *you* (not for your best friend, cousin, or beautician)? Go with that. And don't fret if it's not what you wanted or expected. Hair grows back and styles can be changed. There's no shame in trying something new. The most important thing isn't what other people think about your appearance; it's how you view yourself and feel about you in that hairstyle.

Words to Understand

saunters: Walks leisurely, at an unhurried pace.
sanguine: One of the bodily humors that was thought to determine a person's emotional and physical health, characterized by a ruddy complexion and a courageous, optimistic, and romantic disposition.
melancholy: One of the bodily humors that was thought to determine a person's emotional and physical health, characterized by a gloomy disposition.
phlegmatic: One of the bodily humors that was thought to determine a person's emotional and physical health, characterized by a lack of emotional display and not easily worried, excited, or annoyed.

chapter 5

Making the Most of Your Body with Clothing

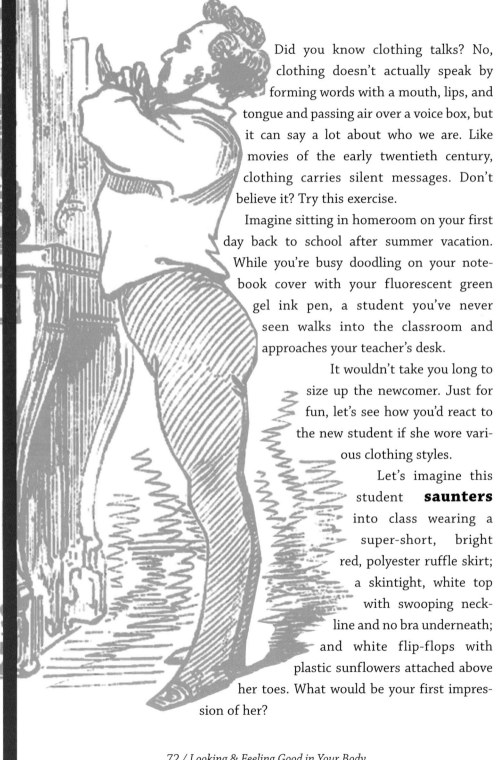

Did you know clothing talks? No, clothing doesn't actually speak by forming words with a mouth, lips, and tongue and passing air over a voice box, but it can say a lot about who we are. Like movies of the early twentieth century, clothing carries silent messages. Don't believe it? Try this exercise.

Imagine sitting in homeroom on your first day back to school after summer vacation. While you're busy doodling on your notebook cover with your fluorescent green gel ink pen, a student you've never seen walks into the classroom and approaches your teacher's desk.

It wouldn't take you long to size up the newcomer. Just for fun, let's see how you'd react to the new student if she wore various clothing styles.

Let's imagine this student **saunters** into class wearing a super-short, bright red, polyester ruffle skirt; a skintight, white top with swooping neckline and no bra underneath; and white flip-flops with plastic sunflowers attached above her toes. What would be your first impression of her?

Now, let's say, instead of wearing the bright skirt and sunflower sandals on the first day of school, she wears black everything: a black tank top with a black mesh overshirt, black oversized cargo pants, black army boots, and black lipstick. Let's throw in a spiked dog collar, an oversized watch chain, and wide black leather wristbands studded with silver. Would you think the same thing of the new student now?

What if, instead of either of the first two outfits, she showed up wearing baggy college-logo sweatpants, a tie-dyed lacrosse T-shirt bearing her old school's name, no makeup, and untied running shoes? What would you think of her then?

How about if she wore capri-length khakis with a brown leather belt, a royal blue button-down oxford shirt, American Eagle flip-flops, light makeup, a Timex watch, a royal-blue hair band to match her shirt, and a Tiffany's sterling silver bracelet?

Your reactions to each of these outfits would differ considerably. Why? Because clothing makes a statement: it reveals our tastes, our attitudes, and our values. The first outfit (short ruffled skirt, tight top) might suggest this girl is boy-crazy or prone to flirting. The second shouts "Goth" and "stay away." The third might imply that she is an athlete, or casual and easygoing. The last suggests "preppy" or affluent or out to make a good impression.

Yes, clothing speaks. The question is, *What are you saying with the clothes you wear?*

Clothing and Personality

The clothing best suited to us will reflect not only our tastes and style senses but will also reflect our "inner self": attitudes, values, feelings about grooming or self-care, energy level, individual traits, passions, and uniqueness. Clothing reveals our personalities.

Author, international speaker, and personality trainer Florence Littauer, in her book *Personality Plus: How to Understand Others by Understanding Yourself* (Revell, 1992), identifies four basic human personality types: the "Popular **Sanguine**" (extroverted, optimistic, likes to talk), the "Perfect **Melancholy**" (introverted, pessimistic, likes to think), the "Powerful Choleric" (extroverted, optimistic, likes to get things done), and the "Peaceful **Phlegmatic**" (introverted, pessimistic, likes to watch). She asserts that though we may see parts of all of these in ourselves at various times, we'll find that one of the four is the most dominant.

In her training seminars, which she gave all over America, Mrs. Littauer mentioned how she can spot each of these personality types in people by observing their clothes. Sanguines consistently like bright, bold, lively colors and fashions; melancholies prefer more subdued, classic, dark-colored looks. Cholerics tend to wear clothes that communicate power; phlegmatics choose subtle, quiet, casual fashions.

Clothing, according to this professional personality trainer, reflects something of who we are. It can also reflect how we feel.

Think for a moment. How do you dress on days when you feel tired, down, or frumpy? More than likely, your clothing will also be frumpy on those days. What do you tend to wear when you feel smart, attractive, or sassy? What you choose to put on will probably match your mood. It may even reflect your confidence.

Clothing and Confidence

Here it is *again*! The confidence thing. Yes, clothing can make a statement about how confident we feel. And clothing, when we use it correctly, can make us feel more confident. It's like a circle that feeds on itself: we dress well—we feel better—we feel more confident—we make better clothing choices that reflect our confidence—so we dress well, and the cycle begins again.

If clothing can make such a powerful difference in our outlook, why is it that so few of us give much thought to our clothing choices? Oh, to be sure, we think about whether or not we look fat, or whether or not a style flatters our figures. And we think about cost. We also think a lot about what's in style right now. But do we really think about our clothing any further than that? Not usually, simply because we don't know how.

According to author, television show host, and personal fashion consultant Leah Feldon, most of us have closets full of clothing that just isn't right for us: some of our clothing doesn't fit correctly, some is ill-suited to our body shapes and sizes, some is outdated, and some simply doesn't match anything else in our wardrobes. We haven't learned to find the clothing best matched to our physiques. We need to learn to find clothing that flatters our natural strengths and camouflages our weaknesses.

How to Find Clothing That's Right for You

First, what color clothing flatters your body best? Newsflash: the most complimentary colors in our wardrobes may not be what we like best. Color Me Beautiful Inc.®, a distributor of high-quality cosmetics, has developed a plan for advising women on what colors to wear based on their hair color and skin tones. Called the Color Me Beautiful guidebook, this system looks at a person's overall physical color attributes and determines which season (spring, summer, autumn, or winter) is closest to her natural coloring, and which colors would best suit her color tones. Women who take the Color Harmony Index evaluation often find that the colors best suited to their skin tones and hair color are not the color choices they would have chosen for themselves.

You can take the Color Me Beautiful evaluation by visiting their website at www.colormebeautiful.com/seasons. In general, if you have light and "cool" hair, your season is summer and you look best in shades of rose, periwinkle, and sage. If you have light and "warm" hair, your season is spring and you look best in shades of turquoise, watermelon, and salmon. If you have dark and cool hair, your season is winter and you look best in black, white, and red. If you have dark and warm hair, your season is autumn, and you look best in shades of moss, rust, and terra cotta.

With all this talk about color, don't forget personality. We saw earlier how personality type can affect our wardrobe choices and what we wear on any given day. What personality traits make you uniquely you? Are you funky? Trendy? Outdoorsy? Artsy? Preppy? Athletic? Casual? Driven? Perfectionistic? Flexible? Low-key? Enticing? Ambitious? Goofy? Feminine? Clothing can, and should, reflect you—not the latest fad and not your best friend. The key is learning to accept ourselves as we are and to give up trying to be someone else. Buy clothes that say "you." You'll feel more comfortable and confident wearing them.

Now that we have a sense of who we are, our likes and dislikes, our quirky tastes, our body size and shape, and we know what colors look best on our skin tones and which styles make us feel most like ourselves, the next most important thing is to find clothes that fit. Yes, fit. It's that simple.

This is how Leah Feldon, the professional style consultant cited earlier, defines a "good fit" in her book *Does This Make Me Look Fat?* (Villard, 2003 paperback edition):

A garment that fits well is neither too

skimpy nor too bulky and is in no way constricting. It falls gracefully and hits your body where it is designed to—not above or below the area. There are no extraneous bumps, lumps, creases, puckers, pulls, gaps, droops, bags, etc. Key areas to watch are shoulders, bust, waist, derriere, crotch, arms, and legs.

How many clothes in our closets actually fit the way Leah Feldon describes? If we're honest, we'll admit that few of our clothes actually do. The author describes several problems with fit that contribute to our looking heavier, overweight, or otherwise less than our best. Here are just a few from her list:

- Tight waistbands: A good fit allows you to place a couple of fingers between your body and the waistband.
- Tight arm casings: Long sleeves shouldn't pull or crease around your upper arms; they should allow free arm movement with no pinching.
- "Smiling crotches": If you can see horizontal lines, creases, or folds across the front of your pants near your crotch, the pants are too tight.
- Pants that cut into your buttocks (either horizontally beneath each cheek or vertically between): This problem is especially obvious in tight jeans and makes us look heavier.
- Clingy knits (tops or bottoms): If you can see every bulge, nook, and cranny, the fabric is clinging too close.
- Gaps between blouse button closures: Shirts that pull across the chest, no matter the bust size, have a fattening effect.
- Skirts that cut under the buttocks: These overemphasize the size of your derriere.

These are just a few, but you get the idea. The point is that in order to look our best and feel our best, we need to wear clothes that fit properly.

Make Connections: Five Tips for Finding Flattering Clothes

1. Know your body type and pick clothes to accentuate your strengths.
2. Know what colors best suit your skin tone, eye color, and hair color.
3. Shop for a good fit. Even the most expensive garment will make you look bad if it doesn't fit right.
4. Make your choice based on fit, not on the numbered size printed on the label. Sizing varies from maker to maker and brand to brand. A size 9 junior in one brand may be the equivalent of a size 13 junior in another.
5. Buy a few quality, well-fitting clothing pieces instead of many cheaper ones.

Above all, choose clothing that moves comfortably with you. When you squat down, bend over, or cross your arms in front of you, your clothing should still feel good on. It shouldn't feel tight or uncomfortable.

Okay, so we've chosen clothes that fit well, reflect our personalities, and compliment our hair, and skin colors. Now what? Accessorize!

Accessories

Clothing, makeup, hairstyles—you'd think that'd be enough to build our confidence. Well, yes, all of these can boost our self-esteem and increase our self-assurance, especially when we learn to use styles best

 Make Connections:
Seven Slimming Style Tips

1. Avoid horizontal stripes, shirts with pockets, double-breasted jackets, and cable-knit sweaters. All of these will make you look broad and bulky.
2. Wear dark, free-fitting, neutral solids that don't cling.
3. Wear clothing with vertical lines or stripes. The only exception is striped spandex pants, which will make you look much larger than you really are.
4. Avoid big prints. If you want to wear prints, look for smaller angular prints, not curvy or swooshy ones.
5. Avoid shiny or stiff fabrics. These accentuate size.
6. Don't wear tight or wide belts.
7. Avoid ruffles, plaids, and pleats.

suited to our bodies. But the makeover isn't complete without finishing touches.

Shoes, belts, pantyhose, socks, handbags, clutches, knapsacks, jewelry, and hair accessories—so many selections from which to choose! Here again keep a few basic questions in mind. What accessories reflect your personality and compliment your overall style and color tones? Which do you like? What looks good on you (be sure to get a trusted friend's honest opinion here)?

The basic rules for accessories are these: "beware of fads" (here today, gone tomorrow); wear shoes and other accessories in styles that match your clothing styles; and, as is true with makeup, less is often more.

Beware of Fads

Fads swoop in one season and are gone the next. By the time you figure out how to wear the latest fad accessory item, it won't be "in" anymore. Just skip it.

Match Shoe Styles (and Other Accessory Styles) to the Style of the Outfit

Shoe styles, unlike clothing fads, change slowly. The biggest shoe mistake we often make is wearing shoes that don't fit the style of our outfits. Wouldn't it look silly to wear a pair of hiking books with a prom dress? Yet we do this, in effect, every day. Try to match your shoe style with your overall clothing effect. If your outfit is funky, wear funky shoes. If your outfit is formal, wear formal shoes. If your outfit is casual, wear casual shoes. Save the hiking boots for hiking shorts or trekking pants.

When wearing short skirts, the standard rule of thumb used to be "the shorter the skirt, the flatter the heel." In today's world of platform shoes, however, this rule seems to have been all but forgotten. Still, it is probably best to leave the platform shoes home when you wear shorty-short skirts. Oh, and one more thing. Never wear pantyhose with reinforced toes when wearing toeless shoes. It just looks tacky.

Less Is More

When it comes to other accessories, just have fun. Make a statement about who you are. But don't go overboard. Designer Isaac Mizrahi once said, "I don't think that tons of jewelry is ever advisable." In jewelry selection, the less is more principle still applies.

Consider chokers. Bulky, wide, or layered chokers make most necks look stunted and thick. For teens and young women with broad shoulders, short necks, and larger busts, this is especially true. Narrow, flat, single-strand chokers, on the other hand, can make the neck look longer. In general, longer necklaces are more flattering to larger bodies, as it elongates the body.

Large beads, bulky costume jewelry, and chunky pendants are more flattering to large bodies than tiny beads and smaller pendants.

Drop earrings and long dangles (kept in proportion to neck length) can make the neck look long and thin. Just don't let the dangles drop past the jawline.

Big, round earrings and bulky button post earrings make wide faces look wider and round faces look rounder. The same can be said of thick, bulky wrist bands on thick arms.

And finally, purses. When it comes to purses, function is probably more important than appearance. Here the less is more rule doesn't apply. Pick a purse that reflects your personality, that will be comfortable for you to use, that can hold what you need to carry, and with which you can have fun. Don't worry about fashion or clashing styles. Just pick the purse that's right for you.

Research Project

Think of a fad that is popular right now. Now go online and see the different fads that have been popular within the last ten years. For example, skinny jeans on men and Silly Bandz were very popular recently. Do any of these fads surprise you or make you laugh? Create a timeline on a sheet of paper, marking which year each of these fads became popular.

Text-Dependent Questions:

1. How can clothing choice reflect a person's mood?
2. What are four reasons that the clothing in your closet may not be right for you?
3. Why shouldn't you follow fads?
4. Why isn't the appearance of your purse as important as the appearance of your clothes, shoes, and accessories?

Final Thoughts About Clothing

Clothing can be a powerful tool in our confidence-building toolbox. It can help us make the most of the bodies we have, no matter our size, shape, color, or even personality. Ultimately, however, to make the most of our bodies (strengths and weaknesses alike) we can't just address the externals of makeup, hair, clothing, and accessories. Making the most of ourselves means becoming the best we can be, from the inside out.

Words to Understand

reprieve: Temporary relief from something.

Chapter 6

Making the Most of Your Inner Beauty: Choosing to Be the Best "You" You Can Be!

Our journey into learning to make the most of our bodies began with the story of an overweight actress who, against the odds, made a name for herself in American television. What we didn't mention when we described Camryn Manheim's many achievements, and what few people know or have heard about, is how many producers, directors, agents, and coworkers in the industry told her that she'd never get anywhere in show business unless she lost some weight.

What made this actress hang in there when everyone told her she'd never make it? How did she ever come to a place where she believed in herself enough, plus-size and all, to pursue her dreams?

In an interview with writer Susan Douglas published in the August 2001 issue of *The Progressive*, Camryn Manheim explains part of how she learned to not only embrace herself, but also to advocate for others:

My parents are activists, and through them I learned to fight for others. But then I learned to fight for myself. Most Americans don't fight for themselves. But we all deserve the same things; we're all equal. You do deserve to be treated with respect. This is not about being entitled. When you're not getting what you deserve, you need to fight for yourself.

I live by the speech Nelson Mandela gave at his inauguration. I have it right here: "Our deepest fear is not that we are inadequate. Our deepest fear is that we are powerful beyond measure. It is our light, not our darkness, that most frightens us. We ask ourselves, who am I to be brilliant, gorgeous, talented, and fabulous? Actually, who are you not to be? You are a child of God. Your playing small doesn't serve the world. There's nothing enlightened about shrinking so that other people won't feel insecure around you. We were born to make manifest the glory of God that is within us. It's not just in some of us; it's in everyone. And as we let our own light shine, we unconsciously give other people permission to do the same. As we are liberated from our own fears, our presence automatically liberates others." [*Note:* Though

in the interview Manheim mistakenly cites the source of this quote as Nelson Mandela's inaugural address in 1994, it appears to have never been mentioned in the address nor is it found anywhere in inaugural documentation. The passage Manheim quoted comes from a book titled *A Return to Love* by American Marianne Williamson, which was released in audio format in 1992 and in print form in 1996.]

Camryn Manheim found strength to accept herself as she was because she knew that as she "let her light shine" it would give others the courage to do the same.

How can we find her kind of courage? How can we learn to accept ourselves just as we are and become all that we can be? First we begin by accepting our body types.

Learning to Love Your Body

The Council on Size and Weight Discrimination has identified ten action steps we can take to better accept and even learn to love our bodies just the way they are:

1. Be around people who accept themselves as they are. Join a support group—or start one if necessary—and talk and listen to others who are on the same path.
2. Read books, pamphlets, and articles on self-acceptance; look at art; and watch films and videos with strong, beautiful characters of different sizes and shapes.
3. Buy full-length mirrors and appreciate yourself from all directions. Look at yourself standing, sitting, from the back, naked, clothed, every way.
4. Buy and wear great clothes you like and feel good in. Get rid of uncomfortable and ill-fitting clothing, and anything you've been saving "until it fits".
5. Take pictures of yourself. Let others take pictures of you. Don't avoid being in group pictures—in fact, insist on standing in the front.
6. Stop being so hard on yourself.
7. Start acting as if you love and have always loved your body.
8. Learn to recognize size discrimination, diet obsession, fatphobia, and body hatred in the world around you—

in advertising, in television and movies, in public accommodations, on the street, and among your family and friends.

9. Start the process of "coming out" as a self-accepting person by telling your family, friends, co-workers, etc. of your decisions: to stop obsessing about your weight and appearance to give up dieting and the goal of losing weight, and to accept yourself and your looks as you are.

10. Become an advocate for the rights of people of any size, shape, color, ability, or physical appearance. Interrupt sizism, racism, look-sism, ableism, sexism, and other prejudiced attitudes wherever you encounter them.

Another important factor in learning to accept our bodies as they are is to shift our focus from weight loss, body measurements, or numbers on a scale to overall health and fitness. The healthiest goal isn't to be thin; it's to be fit.

Making the Most of Your Physical Fitness

No matter what size or shape we may be, we can always take a step or two toward becoming more fit. Small steps and little, manageable changes are key.

Many books, publications, and medical sources supply fabulous information about starting and maintaining an exercise program. We don't need to do that here. However, becoming more active will help you feel better, and as you feel better, your confidence and self-acceptance will grow. Try these things to improve your fitness levels:

Get more active: Take the stairs instead of the elevator. Walk to school instead of hitching a ride. Walk the dog for your folks or neighbor. Use a push mower to cut the lawn instead of a tractor. Ride your bike. Park your car

farther away from building entrances so you can take more steps to get there.

Develop a routine. However you choose to get more active, make it a part of your routine. Do it daily or every other day.

Make fitness fun. People don't stick with activities they dislike. Choose ways of being active that you enjoy. Do you like skateboarding? Make that part of your routine. How about playing drums? Join a marching band. Like to shop? Walk laps at the mall.

Find a partner. Fitness researchers have long known that support and companionship are key to any fitness program. Recruit someone to be more active with you.

Set a goal. Goals can help us with fitness because they keep us on track. Be sure, however, to set realistic goals that you can attain and that are specific enough to identify when you complete them. A specific, realistic, measurable goal would be something like *I will skip the elevator and take the steps at school on Mondays, Wednesdays, and Fridays.*

Reward yourself! If you're making progress with your fitness goals, allow yourself a day off now and then, or treat yourself to that new shirt you've been wanting. Use rewards to keep your incentive going.

Most fitness experts will tell you that exercise alone can't provide total fitness. If we want our bodies to be their best, we need to watch what we eat, too.

How to Make the Most of Your Food Choices

Think about an automobile. If you put good fuel into the gas tank, the engine stays clean, the car runs smoothly, and the car gets better gas mileage. What would happen if you put something other than automobile fuel in the gas tank? The car wouldn't run. What would happen if you watered down the gasoline? The car might sputter and roll a few feet, but it would accelerate very poorly.

It's no different with our bodies. The kind of fuel we put into our "engines" determines how energetic we feel. Good fuel gives us better performance. Bad fuel leaves us feeling sluggish and tired.

What would be good body fuel? You guessed it: healthy foods. What would be bad body fuel? Well, certainly poisons or things that can make us sick. But even food products can be bad for us, especially junk food.

Try these six tips to improve your "fuel economy":

Select serving sizes carefully. It isn't just what we put into our bodies, but *how much* that can help or hurt us. Too little can make us weak and prone to disease; too much can cause us to gain excess weight.

Cut cookies, cakes, and candies. These foods are what nutritionists call "empty calorie" foods. Yes, they provide calories (energy), but they don't provide the vitamins, protein, fiber, or minerals we need to stay healthy. Cakes and sweets don't provide nutrients.

Jettison junk food. Chips, pretzels, caramel popcorn, and other junk foods provide only empty calories as well. We stay healthiest when the calories we consume also provide needed nutrients.

Welcome water. Drinking enough water is vital for feeling energetic and clear-headed. Water also helps our bodies' systems function properly and get rid of bodily wastes.

Feast on fruits and veggies. Fruits and vegetables provide tons of needed vitamins for relatively low calorie costs. Eating lots of them is one way to keep your body as healthy as it can be.

Don't forget dairy. Calcium provides us with strong bones and teeth. Drinking skim milk, eating low-fat yogurt or cottage cheese, or having an occasional slice of farmer cheese (a low-fat cheese) can give us the calcium our bodies need and can help our bodies process protein more effectively.

If we work at becoming more active and focus on making small dietary changes that reflect wiser food choices, we will begin to feel better emotionally and physically. How we think can also play a huge role in our attitudes and outlooks.

How to Make the Most of Your Mind

Just as the fuel we put into an automobile engine affects how it operates, so too the images we stuff into our minds affect how we think.

Imagine if all we ever saw were images of anorexic-thin people. We might be tempted to think that only skinny people fill this world. In fact, as we discussed in earlier chapters, the media already does this to us to some degree. But if that's all we allowed ourselves to see, we'd be feeding ourselves a lie. How much better off we are when we broaden our minds and expose them to images of all forms of beauty and truth found in the real world.

To make the most of our minds, we need to feed our minds healthy thoughts and images, just as we feed healthy foods to our bodies. What we put in our heads impacts what we think and feel. If we read only gruesome thrillers and watch only horror flicks, for example, the pictures we see in our heads will be dark and scary. Or if we only listen to music with violent, self-destructive lyrics, our thought patterns will reflect those patterns. If we, on the other hand, feed ourselves messages of hope and goodness by reading upbeat stories or watching films with heroic characters and messages, our minds and thoughts will be brighter and more optimistic.

The same holds true with the messages we speak to ourselves. If we always criticize ourselves (I'm stupid; I'm ugly; I never do anything right), we'll begin to believe our self-criticisms. The process works both ways, though. If we learn to make positive, life-affirming statements to ourselves (I'm worthwhile; I have something to offer; Yes, I can do this), we'll begin to believe these, instead. Our thoughts and emotions feed on what we put into our minds.

So be positive! Focus on strengths. Tell yourself uplifting truths. Expose your mind to good, positive, hope-filled ideas and stories. Visualize beautiful places. See yourself as loved and needed (you are!). Imagine yourself overcoming your greatest fears and becoming the best you can be. If you see yourself this way often enough, you might just start to believe it.

How to Make the Most of Your Soul

Have you ever wondered why you were born? Have you ever thought about your purpose or the ultimate meaning of life? Have you ever imagined what happened to a loved one after she died? These kinds of questions move us to a deeper place than what our minds and bodies reveal. They remind us that we have a deeper self, a soul.

Have you taken time to listen to the quiet voice deep inside? Have you ever noticed the deeper you? Our deeper selves tend to make themselves known in the quiet of the night, just before we drift off to sleep, or in the early morning hours when we're in that place between sleep and wakefulness, not quite awake but not fully asleep. We become aware of this inner world when loved ones die, when crises come, or when we start to think about purpose. *Why am I here?* is a thought that comes from our souls. The soul is where Camryn Manheim found her courage. We can find courage there, too.

How can we help our souls become the best they can be? Like physical and mental health, we need to learn to care for our inner health.

For centuries, philosophers and religious leaders have known and written about soul care. Regardless of our religions or belief systems, certain practices universally tend to our souls:

Quiet reflection: When was the last time you just sat, stared out a window, and thought about something as big as God, or the universe, or theories of man's beginnings? Have you ever taken time to think through what's *really* important to you or where you'd like to see yourself five years from now? Quiet reflection can calm our inner selves and make us feel more at peace.

Prayer: Whatever your spiritual or religious background, allow yourself some time each day to be reminded of the god or supreme being in whom you believe. Try to talk with him. Talk over the things that are troubling you as if your god were in the room right there beside you. If you're not sure what you believe, it's all right to pray about that, too.

Fasts: Have you ever thought about taking a break from all electronic entertainment for a whole week? That would be an electronic fast. Or how about not eating any dessert for a whole day? That would be a dessert fast. If you chose to give up talking on the phone for twenty-four hours, that would be a telephone fast. We don't have to stop eating completely to fast (although many religious people do). The point of a fast is to change something about your day-to-day lifestyle so that you can focus more on the deeper spiritual issues of life. From what could you fast for a day to give you more time to care for the inner you?

Retreat: Getting away from the busyness of everyday life and responsibilities can reduce our stress levels and help us see life more clearly. Retreats can be as simple as a weekend to the mountains with your family, a morning voluntarily spent alone in your room, or an overnight stay at a camping facility. Retreats are designed to pull us away from regular pressures to give us rest and **reprieve**.

Research Project

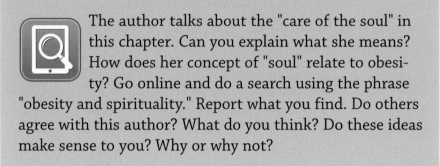

The author talks about the "care of the soul" in this chapter. Can you explain what she means? How does her concept of "soul" relate to obesity? Go online and do a search using the phrase "obesity and spirituality." Report what you find. Do others agree with this author? What do you think? Do these ideas make sense to you? Why or why not?

No matter what your body size, type, color, shape, or appearance, you have a soul, and it needs to be cared for. Sometimes caring for our souls is what finally gives us the courage and perspective we need to allow ourselves the freedom to be who we were made to be.

Free to Be!

Everybody in this world is an imperfect body! We all have things about our bodies we'd like to hide (even the most beautiful among us). When we take time to nurture our bodies, our minds, and our souls, we begin to realize that there are more important things in life than what we look like: health, relationships, love, compassion, world peace, ending human suffering, helping a friend, being kind to a sibling, letting a forgotten grandmother know she's loved. The list is endless.

When we look at our struggles with appearance compared to things like these, it puts things in perspective. Do we all want to be loved? Of course. Do

Text-Dependent Questions:

1. List four things that you can do to improve your fitness level.
2. Why should you exercise with a partner?
3. What are "empty calorie" foods?
4. How does thought affect how you feel physically?

we all want to be accepted? You bet. Do we each want to feel like we have a place and purpose in this world? Absolutely. The good news is that we are and we do! True love, genuine acceptance, belonging, and purpose aren't found in our looks. They are found deep within us. As we embrace the people we are on the inside, we can become all that we were intended to be. If only we'll have the courage to begin.

Why not start now? Don't put it off any longer. Take one action step from this chapter and put it into practice this week. As you start this journey toward making the most of your body, mind, and soul, you'll see your confidence soar and your heart fill with peace. Maybe then you can help someone else begin their journey toward self-acceptance. You can show them the way. As Camryn Manheim quotes, "as we let our own light shine, we unconsciously give other people permission to do the same."

Series Glossary of Key Terms

Aerobic exercise: Activities that use large muscle groups (back, chest, and legs) to increase heart rate and breathing for an extended period of time, such as bicycling, brisk walking, running, and swimming. Federal guidelines recommend that adults get 150 to 300 minutes of aerobic activity a week.

Body mass index (BMI): A measure of body weight relative to height that uses a mathematical formula to get a score to determine if a person is underweight, at a normal weight, overweight, or obese. For adults, a BMI of 18.5 to 24.9 is considered healthy; a person with a BMI of 25 to 29.9 is considered overweight, and a person with a BMI of 30 or more is considered obese. BMI charts for children compare their height and weight to other children of their same sex and age.

Calorie: A unit of energy in food.

Carbohydrate: A type of food that is a major source of energy for your body. Your digestive system changes carbohydrates into blood glucose (sugar). Your body uses this sugar to make energy for cells, tissues, and organs, and stores any extra sugar in your liver and muscles for when it is needed. If there is more sugar than the body can use, it is stored as body fat.

Cholesterol: A fat-like substance that is made by your body and found naturally in animal foods such as dairy products, eggs, meat, poultry, and seafood. Foods high in cholesterol include dairy fats, egg yolks, and organ meats such as liver. Cholesterol is needed to carry out functions such as hormone and vitamin production, but too much can build up inside arteries, increasing the risk of heart disease.

Diabetes: A person with this disease has blood glucose—sugar—levels that are above normal levels. Insulin is a hormone that helps the glucose get into your cells to give them energy. Diabetes occurs when the body does not make enough insulin or does not use the insulin it makes. Over time, having too much sugar in your blood may cause serious problems. It may damage your eyes, kidneys, and nerves, and may cause heart disease and stroke. Regular physical activity, weight control, and healthy eating helps to control or prevent diabetes.

Diet: What a person eats and drinks. It may also be a type of eating plan.

Fat: A major source of energy in the diet that also helps the body absorb fat-soluble vitamins, such as vitamins A, D, E, and K.

High blood pressure: Blood pressure refers to the way blood presses against the blood vessels as it flows through them. With high blood pressure, the heart works harder, and the chances of a stroke, heart attack, and kidney problems are greater.

Metabolism: The process that occurs in the body to turn the food you eat into energy your body can use.

Nutrition: The process of the body using food to sustain life.

Obesity: Excess body fat that is more than 20 percent of what is considered to be healthy.

Overweight: Excess body fat that is more than 10 to 20 percent of what is considered to be healthy.

Portion size: The amount of a food served or eaten in one occasion. A portion is not a standard amount (it's different from a "serving size"). The amount of food it includes may vary by person and occasion.

Protein: One of the nutrients in food that provides calories to the body. Protein is an essential nutrient that helps build many parts of the body, including blood, bone, muscle, and skin. It is found in foods like beans, dairy products, eggs, fish, meat, nuts, poultry, and tofu.

Saturated fat: This type of fat is solid at room temperature. It is found in foods like full-fat dairy products, coconut oil, lard, and ready-to-eat meats. Eating a diet high in saturated fat can raise blood cholesterol and increase the risk of heart disease.

Serving size: A standard amount of a food, such as a cup or an ounce.

Stroke: When blood flow to your brain stops, causing brain cells to begin to die.

Trans fats: A type of fat produced when liquid fats (oils) are turned into solid fats through a chemical process called hydrogenation. Eating a large amount of trans fats raises blood cholesterol and increases the risk of heart disease.

Unsaturated fat: These healthier fats are liquid at room temperature. Vegetable oils are a major source of unsaturated fat. Other foods, such as avocados, fatty fish like salmon and tuna, most nuts, and olives are good sources of unsaturated fat.

Whole grains: Grains and grain products made from the entire grain seed; usually a good source of dietary fiber.

Further Reading

Guevara, Alicia. *Make Up Sense: A Beginner's Guide to Teen Makeup*. Essex, UK: Keyword, 2013.

Natterson, Cara. *The Care and Keeping of You 2*. Middletown, WI: American Girl, 2013.

Shoket, Ann. *Seventeen Ultimate Guide to Beauty*. Philadelphia, PA: Running Press, 2012.

———. *Seventeen Ultimate Guide to Style: How to Find Your Perfect Look*. Philadelphia, PA: Running Press, 2011.

Sparelli, Bella. *100 Natural Beauty Tips That Will Make You Beautiful Forever*. Seattle, WA: Amazon, 2013.

Zelinger, Laurie. *A Smart Girl's Guide to Liking Herself, Even on the Bad Days*. Middletown, WI: American Girl, 2012.

For More Information

About Face
www.about-face.org

Adios Barbie
www.adiosbarbie.com

American Academy of Dermatology
www.aad.org

Body Positive: Boosting Body Image at any Weight
www.bodypositive.com

Campus Blues
www.campusblues.com

Extra Hip
www.extrahip.com

Internet Public Library's Teen Space
www.ipl.org/div/teen

Look Good Feel Better: Programs for Teens
lookgoodfeelbetter.org/programs/programs-for-teens

National Alopecia Areata Foundation
www.naaf.org/site/PageServer?pagename=homepage

National Association to Advance Fat Acceptance (NAAFA)
www.naafaonline.com/dev2

National Eating Disorders Association
www.nationaleatingdisorders.org

National Organization for Albinism and Hypopigmentation
www.albinism.org

Nemours Foundation's Teens Health website
kidshealth.org/teen

Radiance Kids Project
www.radiancemagazine.com/kids_project/kids.html

The Student Center: Teen Fashion
teenfashions.student.com

Teen-Help-Desk.com
www.overweight-teen-solutions.com

Teen Voices On-line
www.teenvoices.com

U.S. Food and Drug Administration's cosmetics page
www.fda.gov/Cosmetics/default.htm

Publisher's note:
The websites listed on this page were active at the time of publication. The publisher is not responsible for websites that have changed their addresses or discontinued operation since the date of publication. The publisher will review and update the website list upon each reprint.

Index

About the Author & the Consultant

Joan Esherick is a full-time author, freelance writer, and professional speaker who lives with her family outside of Philadelphia, Pennsylvania. She is also someone who knows firsthand what it is to struggle with and overcome feelings of inadequacy. She is the author of seventeen books including multiple Mason Crest books for teenagers and her most popular book, *Our Mighty Fortress: Finding Refuge in God* (Moody Press, 2002). Joan has also contributed dozens of articles to national print periodicals.

Dr. Victor F. Garcia is the co-director of the Comprehensive Weight Management Center at Cincinnati Children's Hospital Medical Center. He is a board member of Discover Health of Greater Cincinnati, a fellow of the American College of Surgeons, and a two-time winner of the Martin Luther King Humanitarian Award.

Picture Credits

Alexandragl | Dreamstime.com: p. 66
Benjamin Stewart: pp. 28
Burlingham - Fotolia.com: p. 49
Clipart.com: pp. 10, 17, 20, 21, 37, 41, 44, 47, 51, 57, 75, 87, 98
Dean Bertoncelj | Dreamstime.com: p. 54
Ekaterina Pokrovskaya | Dreamstime.com: p. 62
Ferguswang | Dreamstime.com: p. 22
Hemera Image: pp. 25, 27, 29, 30, 34, 60, 64, 76, 81, 82, 88, 90, 93
Kristina Afanasyeva | Dreamstime.com: p. 72
Maridav - Fotolia.com: p. 70
tro Feketa | Dreamstime.com: p. 84
iy Kobyakov | Dreamstime.com: p. 38
ik | Dreamstime.com: p. 8
p. 12
ediaMicro - Fotolia.com: p. 61

Pulree Library Media Center
1423 West Bryn Mawr Avenue
Chicago, Illinois 60660
(773) 534-2440